Snog, M

By Lisa Holley Palmer
"The Billionaire Matchmaker"

International Award Winning Celebrity Relationship, Dating Expert And Matchmaker.

pink ribbon foundation

Introduction

"The Billionaire Matchmaker"

Lisa has worked with the rich, famous and, on occasion, infamous! She has appeared on mainstream TV, radio and has appeared in countless press articles.

*Lisa is passionate about helping others by adding a sprinkle of laughter and some real home truths, Lisa cuts out the bull**** with true hard cold facts.*

"Lisa Palmer is the Cupid for Millionaires." ***Piers Morgan***

"Lisa is a hugely successful relationship expert and matchmaker."
Anna Bruning, Sunday Times

"Lisa truly is the Billionaire Matchmaker." ***The Creator of X-Factor and Big Brother***

Winner International Businesswoman Awards 2022 ***"Lisa Palmer Relationship Expert".***

CEO Monthly Female CEO of the Year Awards 2022 ***Dating and Relationship Expert Lisa Palmer.***

The reason I think my book is worth reading is I am a qualified award winning dating and relationship expert with the kind of experience that money can't buy! I have put over 20 years of experience and knowledge along with my heart and soul into this book to help you.

Lisa gives us the answers, along with lots of advice, not just about your beau, but about your relationship with yourself.

This book helps you understand all relationships with your family to your work colleagues and your boss, helping you to understand what makes them tick and how they see things in life, to how to communicate with them.

Lisa has interviewed thousands of men and women from all over the world. Lisa gives us advice on ***who to marry and who you must totally avoid.***

How to get confident *and how to be the best version of yourself. With lots of strategies and guidance.*

Lisa tells you all about why ***love raking*** *is so important to know before dating anyone and what deep rooted signs to look for in a man.*

The ***guy you must completely avoid - Mr Atku.***

The ***9 types of men,*** *the good, the bad and the dam right ugly!*

How to communicate with the five different types of ***communication styles*** *and how to understand how they express themselves.*

I have included some of my clients' dating stories (obviously with their permission). They are all true, and I don't doubt that many will make you burst with laughter—or even make you cry.

Find a comfy sofa, a notepad, relax and enjoy.

"You have to destroy a seed to bloom"

-

Lisa Holley Palmer

Table of Contents

Life is like the weather - Lisa Holley Palmer.

Before I start with chapter one, I want you to think about this for the rest of your life.

Life is like the weather, you can't predict it. You certainly can't control it. Somedays you have beautiful sunshine, sometimes there's rain, the rain can be beautiful especially when you see a rainbow, but other times it can cause chaos and disruption.

Then there's the storm which clears the energy. This can also cause destruction, chaos, along with the snow, it looks absolutely beautiful and can be lots of fun. It can also bring change and disruption.

Life is the weather, we change, we grow, we need it to change, although we don't always want the rain or the storm it helps our crops grow and feeds the earth. Appreciate the day and be prepared for the rainy and stormy days, just let it flow and grow like the weather. Remember there is always sunshine after the rain.

Chapter 1: When is a relationship over?

"You cannot start the next chapter of your life if you keep re-reading the last one". - Unknown.

This is a difficult one as sometimes we get so comfortable with each other that we stop trying and it's a very slippery slope and that's why I feel it's so important to have time together or trips away to rekindle that spark.

I personally feel you know deep down if someone doesn't feel right. One of the main signs is if someone is less intimate or not making time or supporting you. If you have stopped talking about the future and making plans together is another indication.

When you still care about each other and those damn emotions get in the way, if you have been together a long time you have emotionally invested time with that person, but that doesn't mean it's the best choice to stay together.

A really good question to ask yourself is where do you see yourself in 5 years? Do you see yourself with your partner?

We grow as a person and sometimes we just outgrow a person and us Brits are good at just staying in a relationship as it's easy and most of us like routine and we know where we are with that person.

If someone is not aligned with your values or stops you from growing, that's not a healthy relationship.

My advice would be to have a little time out from your relationship and ask yourself do you miss that person? Re-evaluate your life and look at your values as these need to be aligned with your partner and do you want the same things in life?

I feel we are on this planet to learn and grow as a person, if someone stops you from growing then it's time to sit down and have that chat as most times when I have had couples see me they actually both feel the same, they didn't want to bring it up in conversation, but do you really want to waste years with someone if they feel unhappy?

I am not for one minute saying part ways, what I am saying is as a couple both people need to be happy, talking is so important so don't sweep it under the carpet.

It's better to have the conversation in the right environment, where you both feel comfortable and you can really talk and get deep and hopefully you can tell each other how you feel and rekindle that spark and grow together, but if you don't you have not wasted more years of your life when you could be with someone who is right for you.

Don't stop growing and life is seriously too short. Learn and grow and be the person you came here to be.

I have added a list of values, look at these and choose at least seven which you feel aligned with. Surely you want someone who invests in you and wants the best for you.

If you do decide to close that chapter, take some time to get to know yourself and be the best version of yourself so you're ready to find someone who is right for you.

You see we mirror what we put out so if you're vibrating you're not feeling great or insecure or not just not loving yourself, you are going to vibrate that energy and attract someone exactly the same, they might not show that first of all, but when you get to know them you will find they feel the same they don't feel great about themselves.

This could go either way. You could grow together and build each other's confidence which is great. You could end up with someone who is very insecure and if you grow, they will start to feel crap about themselves and won't want you to grow and normally tend to see jealousy. Do you really want to go through that?

I feel it is so important when you do start dating to feel great about yourself and love yourself, work on yourself, so you are the best version of yourself!

Core Values:

- Family
- Freedom
- Security
- Loyalty
- Intelligence
- Connection
- Creativity
- Humanity
- Success
- Respect
- Invention
- Diversity
- Generosity
- Integrity
- Finesse
- Love
- Openness
- Religion
- Order
- Advancement
- Respect
- Joy/Play
- Forgiveness
- Work Smarter and Harder
- Excitement
- Change
- Goodness
- Involvement
- Faith

- Wisdom
- Beauty
- Caring
- Personal Development
- This Too Shall Pass Attitude
- Honesty
- Adventure
- Kindness
- Teamwork
- Career
- Communication
- Learning
- Excellence
- Innovation
- Quality
- Commonality
- Contributing
- Spiritualism
- Strength
- Entertain
- Wealth
- Speed
- Power
- Affection
- Cooperation
- Love of Career
- Friendship/Relationship
- Encouragement
- Pride in Your Work
- Clarity
- Fun-Loving

- Charisma
- Humour
- Leadership
- Renewal
- Home
- Be True
- Contentment
- Friendship
- Courage
- Balance
- Compassion
- Fitness
- Professionalism
- Relationship
- Knowledge
- Patience
- Change
- Prosperity
- Wellness
- Finances
- Gratitude
- Grace
- Endurance
- Facilitation
- Effectiveness
- Fun
- Fame
- Justice
- Appreciation
- Willingness
- Trusting Your Gut

- Giving People a Chance
- Patience
- Forgiveness
- Self-Respect
- Abundance
- Reciprocity
- Enjoyment
- Entrepreneurial
- Happiness
- Harmony
- Peace

Chapter 2: Coping with Bad Breakups

"It's never too late to be the person you always wanted to be" - Lisa Holley Palmer

If you're currently struggling to navigate life beyond a breakup, you might feel like nobody's advice is applicable, and no matter how much "self care" you prioritise, nothing truly helps take the pain away.

And unfortunately, well, that's the truth of it. The truest piece of advice that will help you cope after a bad breakup is knowing that time truly heals all. There's nothing anybody can say that will quell the waves of sadness or convince you that it's for the best. Sadness and frustration will linger until suddenly, they won't.

Time Heals All

After a breakup, you're able to distance yourself from the sadness day by day. But sometimes, this doesn't feel fast enough to escape feelings of frustration, jealousy, confusion, or grief that follow a separation. When relationships end, we need time to process and grieve the loss of a person - and a life - we once treasured. As they say, the only way out is through.

When little else offers comfort, know that each day that passes puts you farther from the sadness and closer to a fresh, independent start. How you choose to fill the space between breakup and independence is up to you, and my recommendation is that you fill it with as much joy, reflection, and mindfulness as possible.

How to Fill the Space Between

When you acknowledge the power you have over how you spend the time between a bad breakup and healing, you begin to feel a sense of control over your journey to a healthy, independent state. One of the best ways to spend time navigating your newly-single status is by seeking out activities that make you feel more like yourself. Surround yourself with friends who love you, activities you enjoy, and invest in hobbies that align with your personality. These efforts will help you remain mindful and grounded, contributing to your growth and development in the long run.

By the time you are “out of the woods” of your breakup, you’ll have weeks or months of self discovery to reflect on. Spending time investing in yourself allows you to become closer with the person you’d like to become, and helps you manifest a stronger, healthier.

Chapter 3: The perils to look for when dating

"Something beautiful can come out of a mess" - *Lisa Holley Palmer*

I generally write lots of advice about dating and having fun, but I thought I really should write something about abuse and the red flags and I pray this never happens to you, but I think if you are aware of the red flags or just have the information in mind for future or perhaps your living through this at the moment and have no idea what to do.

When you start dating it's a wonderful warm feeling and it's as if your new partner could do no wrong, but you really do need to be careful. It's best to put your barriers up when you're first dating and try not to drink much as this will blur your vision of your new partner.

Really listen to the conversations and take your time. You see the abuser is very good at manipulating you and I am not for one minute saying everyone is like this as there are some beautiful kind people out there but also there are some real horrors.

Be alert and one of the best ways is when you first go on your date listen to your senses as they will tell you, have you ever walked into a room and felt you didn't quite like someone and you don't know why? That's what your senses are telling you! So really listen to your body.

Listen to the conversation, are they blaming others for their problems? Have they been stopped seeing their children but have great excuses that weren't their fault, I am not saying they are lying but act with caution, another red flag is if you pick up the children and they make you wait so you can't see the ex, again just act with caution it might be genuine but also they might be trying to keep you away from the ex for a reason, so they can't talk to you.

Does your new partner want to be with you constantly and are they acting jealous and possessive? This could be because they are insecure or they might just want to be with you, but it is another red flag to act with caution.

Some people have a bad temper but blame it on something or someone, you will see a pattern that happens regularly, if they are verbally abusive again another red flag.

The types of abuse can vary from physical, emotional, financial, sexual and psychological to include controlling coercive behaviour and can have a devastating long-term effect on victims and survivors as well as their children and families.

My nan said this to me when I was a young girl and it always stuck with me, Lisa, animals have six senses and if the animal doesn't like them, Lisa, get rid of them. LOL. But actually, she was right.

Generally, you may find some abusers are unkind to animals and animals don't like them. You see them growl or they won't be affectionate to that person. Not everyone is unkind but it's just a red flag.

If you have been in a relationship and have reason to believe this person could be abusive, you can find information on this person, it's called Clare's Law, it is a domestic violence disclosure scheme that gives you information from the police if your partner has been abusive or violent in the past. The scheme has two elements: the "Right to Ask" and the "Right to Know".

If records show that an individual may be at risk of domestic abuse from a partner or ex-partner, the police will consider disclosing the information.

This information will take a few days at least to process, so if you feel in danger keep away from this person until you have had this information come back.

Also, remember to clear your web history as a lot of the time controlling relationships and abusers will be looking at your laptops and phones so change all of your passwords or perhaps have face recognition so they can't use your gadgets.

If he or she is an abuser there is lots of help out there it's free. I have added a few charities for you, but again just stay calm and let people know where you are. These charities are incredible. They deal with it daily, so they will know how you feel and will hold your hand and help you.

I have lots of information in my other book The D Word when he's go to go he's got to go. This is not a plug for my book, but it's the reason I wrote it to give you advice from legal advice to getting out of a relationship, financial advice to also advice on how to help your children and how to speak to them and coping strategies for you to help heal yourself.

The experts are best in class from Lawyers to financiers, and psychologists, child psychologists. If you are in immediate danger, always call the Police on 999 or use the silent call system 55 when prompted to raise the alarm and get help.

Women's Aid

Men's Advice Line

Sharan Project

Refuge

Harbour

Shelter

There are lots of charities, these are just a few but there will also be one in your area.

Stay safe Lisa

Chapter 4: How can you tell if your partner is lying to you?

"The purpose of our lives is to be happy" - Dalai Lama.

Relationships are very difficult and one of the key elements of any relationship is TRUST.

My motto is to never lie! Honesty is always the best policy. You run the risk of ruining everything because, eventually, the truth is always revealed.

I suppose you could say that my line of work being a Matchmaker is pretty different to your average nine-to-five, but just as in any industry, it's vital to have the right contacts and know the right people. We all have invaluable experiences to share, and by helping others, we also build trusted friendships that last forever.

Take Darren for example; Darren Stanton is the UK's TV body-language expert and human lie detector. He's always given me brilliant advice on how my clients can present the physical side of themselves to get the optimum effect.

This is something that Darren told me that I want to share with you: "The easiest way to build rapport and a connection with another person, especially on a date, is what experts call matching and mirroring," he says. "This means that you simply match the body language of the other person in terms of what they do with their hands, how they fit. If standing, are they standing on both feet or with weight on one foot over the other? All of this stuff counts."

"As you talk to them, after a few minutes of conversation if you subtly change something small about your body language—for example, if they had their arms crossed and you matched them, you might like to uncross your arms and see if they do the same. The simple answer is that if they do, this means they feel relaxed and connect with you."

This was all a revelation to me. Who knew you could learn so much about someone by just watching tiny gestures of their body and using the same gestures to give them the same subliminal messages?

Something I had always wondered about was how much eye contact to give on a date. Surely you can give too much—and possibly not enough too? Darren's opinion on this is fascinating.

He says, "Normally eye contact is about three to five seconds before a person begins to feel uncomfortable and needs to break contact for a second or two. If the person you are talking to is happy to maintain eye contact beyond the five-second period, then that is another great sign that they are into you and attraction is growing."

There was something else I needed to know. It was the burning question that I've always wanted the answer to—how about being able to tell when someone is potentially lying to you?

Darren told me straight, "Well, telling a lie to avoid social awkwardness is quite normal. For example, telling someone that the birthday present they just brought to you is fantastic when you really think it is terrible is quite normal.

“Generally, people tend to tell darker lies in an attempt to manipulate you into saying or doing something that they want. If the other person is trying to tell you something like ‘I did not cheat on you,’ then they will forget things like their normal hand gestures—and ways of sitting and speaking."

“They will also overcompensate the amount of eye contact they usually give you because they are trying to convince you they are being truthful. It’s more commonly regarded that a liar cannot look you in the eye."

“Listen too for what they say as well as what they do; sarcasm is very often a good indicator as to whether someone is being truthful with you or not.”

I hope this helps you when picking your next partner and for more information on dating and lying Darren has written in my other book the secrets to what men really want.

Chapter 5: Law Of Attraction And How To Manifest A Great Relationship

"The healthiest response to life is joy" - Deepak Chopra

My colleague Arthur Cassidy C.Psycholo, Ph.D, AFBPsS discusses the laws of attraction:

Arthur Cassidy writes:

As a university lecturer in psychology, one of my jobs was teaching modules on the "Science of Love and Attraction" which raises the question conceptually, what is attraction, and is it a universal law?

We agree as psychological scholars that based on objective scientific evidence, we, as humans can experience the joys of love, sex, and harmony in a relationship providing it is based on compatibility of attitudes, likes and dislikes, core beliefs, and salient personality factors.

The law of attraction in the psychological context means that we are socially motivated to seek out those with whom we might find equity, in that we will ideally share similar core values, beliefs, and tolerance, with agreeableness, adventuresomeness, social adjustment, and so on.

At the level of introspection, we know who we are in terms of our personal identity and authentic self as positive individuals open to exhilarating social scenes and with sufficient extroversion skills to find any potential positively oriented partner on earth's radar. Birds of a feather do in fact flock together, and we have a plethora of scientific evidence to confirm that positive people will find longevity and the joy of happiness when they secure a loving relationship with a synchrony of likeable opposite-sex partners. Scientists argue that ethologically, the males will be motivated to procreate with those that satiate his inner physiological and psychological needs. There is a dominance associated with this classical model of attraction and its universal laws. Often we find that opposites attract as we now see a rise in inter-racial relationships across cultures.

Arguments do exist in that the LOA is a falsity, imbued with idealistic thinking patterns and anecdotal experiences that amount to a metaphysical phenomenon without factual substance. However, the LOA is more than generalisations. Thinking about an Aston Martin or the latest Ferrari, it is argued, triggers off the decision-making apparatus in the brain's emotional centre - the amygdala, motivating you to make wise investments and to keep focused on sitting on those plush cream leather seats with the perfect partner beside you. Live your dream we exclaim with alacrity!

However, here are some reasons why there is no such thing as LOA... Let me tell you that it is metaphysical pseudoscience as its conclusions are based on erroneous, unconfirmed, and pure assumptions devoid of any scientific methodology or expertise. The LOA has no purpose nor has it a concrete plan. However, it claims that you ought to see yourself as already having the things you want. I desired a stunning Texan woman with legs like an antelope and a wide mouth with full red lips fronting an array of perfect teeth like a piano keyboard. I never found her. It further argues that if I see myself as adventurous with the opposite sex filled with prowess, creativity spontaneity, animal instinct, and pheromones ablaze from my armpits, I'll be the happiest man alive. We have to be sceptical as nature versus nurture theory dictates that our attraction will ultimately depend not just on genetics and DNA, but how we have been influenced by our parents and peers, our own moral reasoning, and core values and beliefs.

Lisa Holley Palmer writes:

As a relationship expert and matchmaker who has worked with Hollywood stars, royalty, and businessmen and women, I have interviewed thousands of successful people and believes that the laws of attraction can work in both love and life, so just as you might set about finding a partner in business or doing business with people you like, you might apply the same rules when looking for love.

Instead of hoping someone will turn up, one way you can speed the result up is to manifest a relationship. But before you start that process you need to start within, you need to love yourself, you need to be honest with yourself and feel happy and fulfilled inside and out as people are attracted to the same kind of people.

Let's concentrate on finding a new interpersonal relationship. The following list illustrates the five main things that hold people back. I call them The five stone-cold killers

1. You have been cheated on
2. You are feeling rejected

3. You are body conscious or worried about your weight
4. You have hang-ups about your physical appearance, teeth, loss of hair, possible scarring, or other
5. Education, you feel you are inferior

Which one of these five points is making you feel bad about yourself and holding you back? Perhaps it's one or more of the above.

I cover points 1 and 2 separately below because in my experience these two are often the most painful to deal with and can be very debilitating over time.

Points 3, 4 & 5 are relatively easy to deal with, believe it or not, and can be fixed with a good dose of willpower, a clear plan, and in some cases, expert help and advice.

Human beings, unlike any other creature on this planet, have the ability to see things before they happen, they also have a unique ability to change course in any direction at any moment. Take for instance the house that you live in, someone (and it may have been you) decided to build that house, in their mind's eye they saw the finished property, its character, size, orientation, and environment. Once they had created it in their mind's eye they set about making it a reality.

What they didn't do is wander onto the property and start laying bricks with no clear plan of what they were going to build.

You see, we have an amazing ability to visualise what we want and then create a clear plan to achieve our goals. Set you're love goals.

Point 3. If you are worried about your weight, create a plan, follow a program (there are many great books available as well as free YouTube videos), we have lots of advice form experts on (www.mogullove.com) which involves eating the right foods and exercise, add a dollop of perseverance, and watch the weight fall off.

Point 4. Appearance, whatever it is you want to change, start off by firstly making the best of what you currently have. Next, set about making a plan to get what help you need and from whom, write this down. Put a timeline on this. You may need to earn some extra money and if this is the case, work out how you will do this, how much you need, and when you will have hit your target.

Education, in this day and age in the UK we are blessed, not only do we have libraries covering next to everything you might want to learn which are completely free, we also have amazing access to the internet for online learning. Wherever your education is today it does not have to stay there. Create a plan of what you want to learn and work on your plan. Learning anything is like building a muscle. It's all about repetition. If your weakness is written or spoken English, Maths, History, or Quantum Physics all you need to know is available today and mostly free to read or watch.

Hey, I just had a thought, imagine how you would feel in 12 months if you worked a weekly plan on all three!!!!

So how do we deal with the problem of rejection or being cheated on.

DEALING WITH REJECTION AND BEING CHEATED ON

Rejection: firstly is it real rejection or is it perceived rejection and perhaps it does not exist? How someone reacts to what they think is rejection is often steered by past experiences and how they are currently feeling.

You may be married to someone who has been rejecting you, the person has decided to move on and actually it's only a matter of time before they end the relationship you unfortunately just don't know that. As hard as this is often you have to decide to move as there is little point being in a relationship with someone who does not want to be with you, this hurts like hell. Perhaps this is where you have now arrived and it is the main reason you have had enough and calling the marriage off.

How do you actually know this is the case and your partner wants to move on? The best way (which is also the most painful) is to confront them calmly, tell them how you are feeling, ask them to tell you why they are acting the way they are, and then give them an easy way out of the relationship. Here is the thing if they are going to leave they will take your offer there and then or they will say they need to think things through and normally they will call things a day in a day or so and say the relationship is over. Horrible I know but you need to know, life is short and you need to build your life on solid foundations.

However, sometimes it takes a conversation like the one I have described to give your partner a jolt and re-evaluate your relationship and how they feel about you. Sometimes your partner is possibly rejecting you because your relationship has gone stale or perhaps you are being too controlling. I hope that if this is the case you can improve your communication and work on this together.

Being cheated on: There is no getting over this quickly it's horribly painful and emotionally crushing.

You feel rejected, angry, sad, scared, and empty all at the same time.

You have 2 options and neither are easy,

1 End the relationship and move on as fast as you can. This is much easier if you are single or in a relationship where children are not involved. You might be heartbroken but the trust has gone and there is no way back for you.

2 Try and find a way of forgiving your partner. In my experience this can only happen if you know all of the facts, your partner has been honest about why it happened and you have decided that you believe that it was a one-off and the relationship is worth fighting for.

It's easy to judge other people's lives and from experience, I can tell you the circumstances around cheating can vary widely. Let me give you two scenarios, firstly, your husband, wife, or partner has never cheated on you, is very loving, and has always been loyal.

They go out with friends and drink too much, so much so they actually cannot remember their actions and they have a one night stand, they are mortified and either confess or you find out. Whatever the scenario, they have never done it before and made a huge mistake. The second scenario is your partner has been having an affair for months or even perhaps years it has been planned and is calculated.

When you look at the two scenarios you will see why things are not as black and white as it may seem.

Forgiving does not mean forgetting but you must forgive to make it work. You cannot say you are going to forgive and then keep throwing it in your partners face every time you get angry because that will not work for the long term

Do the following exercise,

1 Take personal time out, grab a journal, and make notes about what is good in your relationship.

2 Make notes about what has not been working of late and why. Don't blame yourself for their infidelity but do look back and try to notice where things might have started to slip.

3 What habits your partner has that are no longer acceptable to you and they must change or you cannot move forward.

4 What you would like to change about yourself and what action points are needed (This is not about you negatively beating yourself up, quite the opposite, what strengths and character traits do you now want to adopt).

5 Speak to 5 best friends/family members and ask them what they truly think about your partner (try and split this up between two groups who aren't close to each other). Ask them to be very blunt, make notes, and take time out to consider what your nearest and dearest are saying. If they tell you things are worth fighting for this will help you but if they all say run a mile this person is very bad for you and can't/won't change then you probably need to run a mile.

A word of warning some people will never change it's just not in their DNA and this reminds me of the story of the scorpion and the frog:

There was a scorpion and a frog, sort of friends walking along a riverbank one lovely sunny day and they eventually reach a point where they can go no further and the only way to get to where they want to go is to cross the river. The scorpion looks at the frog and smiles, the frog says politely what are you smiling for and the scorpion says great news you are a great swimmer so I will jump on your back and you can get us both to the other side.

The frog looks at the scorpion and says "look I am not sure I want to do that because you are a scorpion and if you sting me I will drown to which the scorpion says, "don't be stupid if I sting you we will both drown because scorpions can't swim" so the frog thinks good point that would be truly a stupid thing to do.

The frog says to the scorpion hop on I will get us across and the scorpion obliges, halfway across the river the frog feels terrible pain and realises the scorpion has stung him and they are both going to drown. The frogs look at the scorpion and say why did you do that? We are both going to die to which the scorpion says I'm really sorry I couldn't help myself, it's in my nature.

Finally, take your time, and do not make rash decisions, stay off social media, and do not ever lower yourself to revenge, never blame yourself and do not feel embarrassed.

I am 100% for marriage and long term relationships but choose them wisely.

Once you have the best version of you, now ready for Law of Attraction, and this can work both in business and looking for a new partner. Put your list together and visualise how it looks like and feels.

And don't change to please other people or try to change to fit in. You only ever change for you and you alone!

Lastly, I have a mantra which I have for myself personally and my business which I use every day: "Right thoughts, right word's, right actions." Start your's today and the best of luck.

Chapter 6: How to have a successful Relationship

"Life is a flower of which love is the honey" - Victor Hugo

Dating is not always easy, so many of us have anxiety about dating and it's not surprising because of the stories you hear and past relationships that might not have been so kind.

I am going to be brutally honest with you, if you say you were in an awful relationship what did you learn from it? If you didn't learn anything then there is possibly something wrong with yourself. I know it's harsh. We all need to look at ourselves too and take some responsibility in some cases and look at what happened and why it happened, it's just a small tweak we need to change to improve our dating life.

IF YOU ARE WAITING FOR SOMEONE TO COME AND SAVE YOU OR FIX YOU DON'T! YOU ARE RESPONSIBLE, YOU HAVE THE POWER TO MOVE YOUR LIFE FORWARD. NO ONE IS COMING TO SAVE YOU, BUT YOU.

What can you do? One of the best ways to get answers is to ask yourself the question: WHY? you see we all know the answers within, so be on your own and go over the relationship why did it end, or why did that happen? If you don't know the answer, get your journal and write WHY until you get the answer. You will get the answer and once you have it then look at the why and start working on yourself.

You see we are a mirror and what's in our mirror we reflect, you will get what you are putting out there. So if you are not feeling good about yourself or you are unhappy. You will get the person who feels the same, that's why I have always said to my clients you must take time out after a relationship has ended and re-evaluate what happened good and bad as we are all here on this planet to learn life's lessons. Once you have evaluated those issues, work on those things and be the best version of yourself and you will then attract a similar person who will be the best version of them.

Anxiety is worry about the future, but if you have worked on yourself and when you have done this you will feel you are the best version of yourself then you should feel you hardly have any anxiety. We are all going to have slight nerves and a little apprehensive that's natural, but there is only one you! So be proud of who you are and don't let anyone dampen your sparkle.

I truly want the best for you!

Chapter 7: My mess at the mansion got me literally dumped.

"Keep smiling because life is a beautiful thing and there's so much to smile about" - *Marilyn Monroe.*

Talking about first dates, let me tell you a story about one of my male clients I introduced to one of my female clients. It's hilarious; now it's the main story at all of his dinner parties.

A client of mine has IBS. It's horrible for him, but he copes as well with it as anyone can. A couple of years ago he went for a date quite soon after meeting this girl who was very wealthy and, in his words, stunning.

When she invited him to her beautiful home, he knew that he was going to have to really dress to impress and act the part. As he predicted, it was an incredible house, and he was almost too scared to touch anything. The place was immaculate.

He was also quite nervous, so he told her he needed the loo. Unfortunately, one of the main symptoms of IBS is the possibility of loose bowels in anxious situations, so he expected that he might need the toilet at some point. He had learned over the years to control it, but he knew at that moment he was in trouble.

Whilst rushing to the toilet, disaster struck. All of a sudden, he had an uncontrollable bowel movement. He could feel that it had gone horribly wrong; he knew he was in trouble and urgently needed to get to the toilet to clean himself up.

He was frantic, and because the house was so huge, he got lost on his way back from the bathroom. Panicking like mad upstairs, he wasn't thinking straight and made a bizarre decision—to throw his underwear out of the front window, thinking he would try and pick them up when he left as he didn't want to walk back downstairs with the smelly pants. Sounds like a good plan? No!

It didn't work out that way. He was mortified to discover that he didn't throw them out of the front of the house, but out of the back of the house and on top of the conservatory roof. They were lodged there and beyond retrieval. So, the soiled, stinking pants stayed there—and guess what? He never heard from or saw her again!!

My motto in this story is to try to relax! We all get tense on dates, and if we like the person, we can get ourselves tied up in knots. But honestly, it does us no good at all. Just be you as you are perfect just the way you are!

Chapter 8: - The worlds shortest fairy tale

"If you love life, don't waste time, for time is what life is made of." - Bruce Lee

I got this joke through from my male friend Jonathan and it did tickle me, so the joke said:

The world's shortest fairytale

Once upon a time, a guy asked a girl "Will you marry me?

The girl said, No!"

And the guy lived happily ever after and rode his motorcycle and went fishing and hunting and played golf a lot and drank beer and scotch and had money in the bank. And left the toilet seat up whenever he wanted.

The End.

I hope that made you laugh and men if you're reading this put that bloody toilet seat down LOL.

In all honesty and as an expert it's really healthy for relationships and marriages to have healthy time apart to do the things you like to do, I see quite a few clients who were unhappy as they were trying to keep their partner happy but actually when you talk to both parties they were both unhappy as they would work but didn't make time for themselves and to have a happy healthy relationship you need to be happy so try to make time at least once a month if not more, time for you and have a day off from your children and partners and your find it will bring a spark in your relationship and gives you something to talk about.

Just a little fact for you, men communicate on average around 7,000 words a day while women tend to communicate about 20,000 so we both need our own space and time with friends. It's all about balance. Balance in a relationship is so healthy and it's about making sure there’s independence, and communication and this will help your relationship thrive.

Chapter 9: Are you being love-raked?

"For every difficult situation, there is always a lesson and hope". - Lisa Holley Palmer

Are you being Love Raked?

Power and Control in a relationship: What are the signs? How can we change this behaviour?

Every relationship someone generally takes control of the finances or taking responsibility for the choirs, children, food shopping etc. I understand that every relationship is different and we all have different schedules and responsibilities and that's normal.

When is the power becoming controlling?

Generally the first sign of controlling is stopping you from seeing family and friends or going out. This is not acceptable. No one should control you, the only person who gets to control you is **YOU**. Here is a few more signs of controlling:

These are as follows:

Emotional Abuse is an act that subjects someone to behaviour that could result in fear, anxiety, depression and character assassination and presuming your guilty. Public embarrassment where they make an example of you in public and ridicule you. Giving no regard to your thoughts and feelings. Treating you like a child

Using children I know some dads have lost access to their children and again unless there is a valid reason, it's so healthy for children to see their dads, even if you can stand your ex, it's not your children’s fault.

Threats, like leaving you or cutting off privileges and making you feel so stuck in a relationship you stay out of fear. (If this is the case please see my book:

The D Word, it will give you all the information to help you move on with a plan).

Using Economic abuse this is one of the most used forms, controlling your bank and how much you have to spend, to where you are going each day and checking your mileage and your phone, and alarming amount of calls finding out where you are all the time.

Chronic criticism the way you dress, to the way you speak, to the way you eat and what you eat. This is not acceptable.

Using Guilt as a tool, Many controlling people are skilled manipulators and use this to make their partner feel guilty and this makes the partner give up their power, which plays right into the controllers hands.

Take back your power, but you must do this as long as you're not in a violent relationship. Again if this is the case The D Word has lots of advice and charities that can help you. If you have nowhere to turn to please dm me on instagram - Lisa Holley Palmer and I can point you in the right direction.

Sometimes what happens is a partner will be overly nice to you and they will shower you with gifts and affection. They are love raking you! So you feel loved and secure, then a few days later it turns into uncontrollable rage and you are walking on egg shells. Your emotions are feeling all over the place, from one day to the next, as you never know what you are coming home to.

Don't get me wrong, everyone has a bad day. You might come home grumpy and upset, you might have a row, but when it's constant this is emotionally exhausting and you become drained. And little by little you lose your identity. You need to realise this is a person taking your control and power.

These are some signs to look out for:

They overreact at the smallest thing and become overpowering, you tend to see it when you're in the car and they get uncontrollable road rage.

- They brag or boast about themselves.
- They seem to be insecure or uncomfortable around other people.
- They always need your support emotionally.
- They seem to have a chip on their shoulder about how bad everyone has treated them.
- They make all the decisions for you.
- They are possessive of you, acts of jealousy.

If you are man or woman I have seen women control men too, it's a two way street. So how can you stop controlling behaviour?

How to Stop Being Controlling in Your Relationship:

- Self- esteem is key
- Acknowledge therapy
- Practice self-care
- Learning to value and love you
- Being clear with expectations and setting boundaries.
- Ask yourself what you hope to achieve from your control?

A few ideas to help you if you are the controller:

- Do what you enjoy and bring you happiness so you lose track of time.
- Therapy people see this as weakness, I see this as strength as owning your behaviour and you should be proud of yourself.
- Physical exercise is really important
- Eating healthy as this can really affect your mood.
- Spend time outdoors being in the daylight for an hour at least being in nature, and in the

winter as we don't see much sunlight and taking supplements that lift your mood, like Vitamin B,C and D.

From most clients I have seen, the control from relationships stems from childhood and seeing their parents pattern or low self esteem.

It's not always the persecutors fault they don't know how to stop it or change. I have added a few things that can help, if this is still a problem therapy tends to be the answer or talking through with a trained specialist, because they can get to the root cause quickly and effectively.

Low self esteem is probably the most common.

You will need to start building on your relationship with your partner to bring back that closeness again and here is some examples, how to do that:

- Showing an interest in the things they like and join in if you can.
- Working out together or walking in daylight and nature will make you feel good and give you quality time together.
- Learn what makes your partner happy and everyone is different.
- I will give you a few examples:

- Perhaps your partner love's physical touch and cuddling is great!
- Your partner has always had a list of odd jobs to do, fix the toilet seat or perhaps he wants you to fix his hole in his jeans as some people feel the act of service is the way to their heart.

- Maybe it's just quality time together, as having children is a wonderful thing, but don't get me wrong they can be a pain in the a**e sometimes and you need healthy times for your relationship.
- Your partner feels loved through gifts, a bunch of flowers or a new tie, whatever it is, they feel loved with a small act.
- Some people are auditory and need a sense of words, so telling them you love and cherish them makes this type or person feel good.

Good luck, remember we don't come with a remote control, balance is key.

Chapter 10: Feel your relationship has lost its spark

"If you don't like the road you're walking, start paving another one". - Dolly Parton

Try the new dating fad that is proving to be the saviour of the modern-day relationship.

Feel you've lost your spark? Need to, in the words of Take That, relight your fire?

I see so many unhappy clients who feel they have lost the spark and aren't sure where to turn. Many couples give up too easily these days with the divorce rate at 13 an hour in the UK as the USA is 277 per hour.

It is so easy to fall into a routine and lose the motivation to go out and experience new things together. We've all been in a long term relationship or married to an old grumpy git and thought 'where the hell did the fun go?'

Friday nights have inevitably become the same unexciting sequence of dull events as you both sit at home watching Eastenders whilst he passes gas and flicks through endless television channels before falling asleep on the sofa, attractively (not), catching flies and heavily breathing out the garlic bread you had for dinner (certainly no Brad Pitt).

If you're reading this and have forgotten what a decent sex life is as well. It has got to the stage that you find more excitement through consuming a bar of Cadburys than to make the effort to have sex at the end of a fun-filled, TV fuelled, night in (yawn).

If the above sounds like I have described your relationship, it is time to take action!

Introducing: The incredible Alpha-dating!

Alpha-dating is a way to put the excitement, mystery and fun back into your relationship by going week by week (or month by month) and taking it in turns to go through the alphabet, coming up with a different date beginning with each letter of the alphabet. For example, it could be for archery, get out Cupid's bow and arrow, and put the love back into your life!

And it doesn't have to always be a day/night out, it can be something different in the bedroom or going to a new location for a romantic night away. It's the element of surprise and something you can both look forward to - use your creativity and make it personal!

So many relationships break down as they lack the **3 elements KEY** to a successful and long-lasting bond: **FUN, INTIMACY, and COMMUNICATION**. Get these 3 well balanced and you should stay happy in your relationship.

We all want that first date feeling back, the element of surprise, so don't sit around but get out there and create new memories, new things to chat and joke about and all in all get back to enjoying each other's company.

Have fun with it, wind each other up, play games, give each other a clue or send a few saucy pictures! It's time to ditch the bog-standard 'date night' that often never happens and hit the new, modern way of dating

Chapter 11: Disastrous first date, the Police, Fire and Ambulance Service and who pays the bill?

"Make today so awesome, yesterday gets jealous" - *Unknown.*

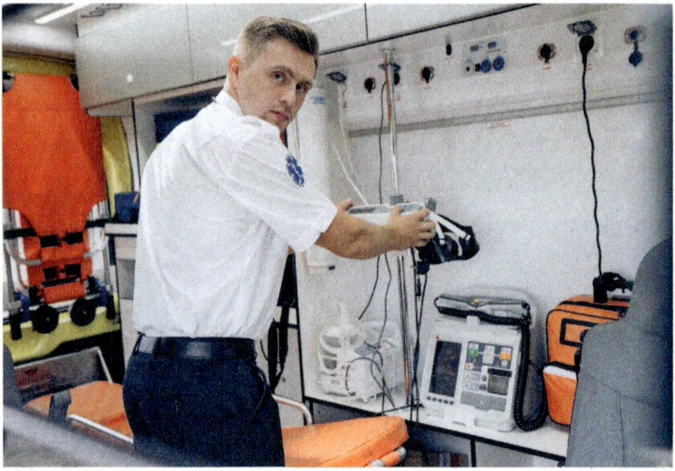

First dates can be fun and you never know what's going to happen... It's interesting as I look after clients from all over the world, and 82% of male clients generally get the bill for the first date as men want to fulfil the role of being a gentleman.

I have been helping a young Ukrainian lady who has never dated anyone from the UK, she said Lisa how does it work? Ukrainian women do not pay the bill at home, but how does it work in the UK?

I believe men should demonstrate that they are financially secure and ready to support you, especially when you are on your first date. It doesn't even mean he'll be doing the same thing on the second date, but it does mean he values you enough to be generous.

I believe it can say a lot about your financial future together and let's face it most women want to be wooed.

So, there I was in my prime and aged twenty-six! The date was set and so exciting. The guy had put in so much effort. We went to a lovely restaurant for a swanky dinner, and yes, believe it or not, I only had one glass of wine. So, I was on my best behaviour well, trying to be, at least! I spent half the day shopping for a new outfit, and hours getting ready and feeling good. I felt like a million dollars as I left my house.

We had gone to a fishing village, called Pevensey Bay. It was a stunning evening in late summer, so we thought we would have a romantic stroll along to Pevensey Castle. Unfortunately, on arrival, I had an idea that might not have been one of my best.

This idiot—moi—decided to be nosey and climb on top of the wall to see if we could have a peek at the castle, which sat behind the wall. Sounds like a good idea, right? What could possibly go wrong?

As I attempted to straddle the wall, I slipped and fell close to twenty feet. It was a little bit like Del Boy in *Only Fools and Horses* when he falls through the bar flap, if you have ever seen the episode (series 6 episode 1, "Yuppy Love"). As people say, you could not have made it up!!

I was mortified, embarrassed and very, very sore. The police turned up with the fire brigade and an ambulance. Then the firefighters were sent down to help the ambulance men to get me on a stretcher and pull me out with the fire engine. (No, I am not that big a unit! I was a long way down!)

I wanted the ground to just swallow me up there and then. But the police needed to ask me a few questions...

"Ms Palmer, this castle has been here since 1066, built by William the Conqueror to keep people out, and no one to our knowledge has ever fallen down. How long have you been down there?"

For once in my life, I was stunned into silence. I hadn't even been there for two hours. The next thing I knew, I had to go in the ambulance for X-rays at the hospital.

I was very lucky—a ruined outfit, a few bruises, ego crushed, and, you guessed it, I didn't see the guy again, although he seemed a lovely man! Ladies, best tip: Always wear good underwear when you go abseiling.

So, first dates can be fun. If I didn't go, this would never have happened, and at least the story always makes people laugh!

Who knows what's going to happen on your first date? Just don't be nosey like me if you can help it! On the plus side of my embarrassing experience, I did get to see some rather tasty firefighters, so no complaints there.

So, back to the first date. Many people ask me what to do at the awkward part when the dreaded bill comes.

Men are funny creatures (plenty of my clients have other not-so-funny names for them). The best thing you can do is always offer to buy them a drink at the start of the date.

It's a psychological thing. Most men will say no; nearly all will be prepared to pay for dinner. Worst case, ladies, and do be prepared—you might need to go Dutch. Embarrassing, but you might need to split the bill.

Call me old-fashioned, but most men don't realize how much you have spent for the bloody date in the first place. New underwear, manicure, new outfit, then the hours of getting ready. All of that takes time and a lot of money! There's no doubt about it—the man should always pay the bill. Not only does it show you that he's a true gent and will look after you, but also when and if you have children, the chances are he will be a generous and supportive father.

Good luck on your date and stay away from any moats!

Chapter 12: Online scammers and deception

"Turn your wounds into wisdom". - Oprah Winfrey.

Here is a short guide as to how you will know how male (and female) scammers work and how not to become spontaneous and sucked in online.

This world of online dating scammers is an international crime at its best. Their motives are to use the ultimate level of con tricks, deception and romance scams to suck your bank account dry and threaten your relationship with family and friends and much more.

The romance scam, as it's popularly known, is where scammers are trained to target you emotionally online by using the following methods. These are online criminals, remember, and they will construct fake profiles frequently using high-definition portrait photos and videos to catch your attention.

Psychologically we are more likely to respond to a high-quality photo image online in contrast to relatively ordinary profile pics.

The scammer will likely be a young male, with extremely good looks well above the average, and will be professionally dressed formally and casually. Danger sign!

There biography is usually minimal with little relevant detail or if there is a biography, the scammer has made so many mistakes as the image portrayed is not consistent with the biography.

Once you allow your emotions to take control, you will begin to enter the "grooming room" and like the fish deep under the river, you rise to grab the bait!

He (or she) will be working from prepared "scripts" where they are motivated to groom you, knowing you are sexually attracted to them and perhaps even aroused physiologically by what you see. This will encourage the scammer to create a "relationship" with you as they know you are vulnerable to their physique, sexuality and lifestyle, and more. Watch out!

Their responses to yours will often not be instant as they are dealing with several "clients" at the same time. They will not answer any questions you ask them, another giveaway sign, but will get angry if you persist in asking questions. Scammers will then after three or four days, intensify their grooming by telling you about their broken phone, or relative, a son or daughter in the USA or they need money for a specific job they have to do and will tell you that they are out of work due to an illness.

If you sympathize with the phone story, as you may be extremely vulnerable, you might just send them your spare phone and go to the trouble of getting it unlocked and factory reset, just so they can use it to communicate with you, and so on.

The motive is to gain your sympathy by playing on your emotional functions. Stop right there!

You have seen several red flags and take it from me. Delete your account immediately. Go back and review the sessions you had with your psychologist or therapist and review all the sensible skills you learned. These scammers lure you into sending a small amount of money e.g £100.00 to gain your "trust." Once anyone is foolish enough to do this, they win you emotionally by promising to pay you back when you meet in person… which never happens.

Incidentally, they may and often do ask you to send them a pic or rather a "hot topic" semi undressed or partially naked photo, and emotionally vulnerable women who do this may find the scammer will use this to blackmail you if you refuse their extra demands for money.

They will never allow you to see them on a video call to you and will want to get off the dating site texting asap so as to leave no trace there of their conversations and demands. If you carefully listen to them there is often background noise as many operate in rooms similar to internet cafes. They can never follow a proper conversation with you and often forget what you and they talked about yesterday or a few hours ago.

The aim is to build up your sexual arousal brain mechanism where you become psychologically dependent on seeing them morning afternoon and evening.

A more recent ploy is for them to make alluring aerobic videos at home in designer gear and send them to you as part of the allure. Back to reality and within the first fifteen minutes ask to see them on a video call or block them and report them and the conversation to the registered owners of the dating site.

Scammers are very sophisticated and use model pics constantly to attract anyone who they feel has money in the bank after a divorce settlement or redundancy payments.

You can also check them out by taking a copy of their online pic and putting it into reverse image check on Google and this should confirm their identity as a scammer.

In summary, be alert and aware of who comes into your circle of friends and acquaintances.

Remember your emotional vulnerability, so never compromise yourself. Avoid online dating activity as it's potentially foolish as you're allowing your emotions to direct your motives and behaviour. Take back proper control of your emotions and develop meaningful relationships with people you know well and their backgrounds. Check and double-check within reason, but don't allow yourself to become obsessive. Stay calm, cool and in control of everything around you. Be empowered to be the person you really want to be. You can do it.!

Dr Arthur Cassidy and Lisa

Lisa write's I also want to add:

My gift to you is always, always listen to your gut. So how do you do this? Have you ever walked in a room and automatically not liked someone you don't know why, but you just know. Well that's your gut/soul talking to you. So when your in a business meeting or on a first date, please listen to your gut the first minute as your gut or should I say your soul its talking to you and no one loves you more or has your back then your soul/gut.

When your next in a room listen to your soul.

I should have listened to mine, but I think that's why I didn't so I was able to write this with the true knowledge and experience, remember charmers, narcissist, they know how to play the game, the soul game I call it, how to trick your soul and take over you. Please don't listen to them, listen to your gut and you will never go wrong.

Chapter 13: First dates: What is important ?

"Your life isn't yours if you always care what someone else thinks" - Unknown

Whether you're new on the dating scene, returning to the dating world after a failed relationship, or just thoroughly enjoying your dating phase of life, there are three very important values that I encourage my clients and connections to maintain when exploring new relationships. It's important to decide on your core values that you want to maintain as you meet new people and make romantic connections.

Your core values as you approach dating will have an impact on the way you perceive others and the way others perceive you, and will also directly affect the amount that you are able to truly connect with another person. The values I encourage others to prioritise when dating are transparency, integrity, and vulnerability. Let's break those down:

Transparency

This value will help you avoid wasting time (yours... and theirs). Being transparent about what you're looking for, what's important to you, and your deal breakers is crucial early on in a new dating relationship.

Take advantage of your first few dates with someone new to be your authentic self, this will give your date a good idea of who you truly are, and if the two of you are not a great fit, being transparent will help this come to light early on.

Integrity

Do not compromise on who you are in order to please someone else. With billions of fish in the sea, there is no reason to fall short of your own principles in order to accommodate a potential partner - trust me when I say there are plenty more options for you out there.

Your integrity shines through as your ability to maintain your other values, and if you can avoid compromising, it'll ensure that you feel confident about the outcome of new encounters regardless of whether or not it works out in your favour.

Vulnerability

Being vulnerable is another way to ensure that you maintain a practical approach to dating new people. Being vulnerable helps your date get vulnerable, too. Vulnerability is where both you and your date will learn the most about each other - fears, values, and what you're both looking for will shine through during your most vulnerable moments.

While it can feel scary, sharing childhood memories, hopes for the future, and reflecting on the past can help you grow closer to someone quickly, increasing the chances that you can determine your compatibility early on.

Stay true to these values as you navigate the potential minefield of dating and you'll find great success!

Chapter 14: Getting you date confident.

"Look for something positive in each day, even if some days you have to look a little harder". - Unknown

For sure you will be feeling nervous, you need to have the right mindset so you ooze confidence. Before reading any further I want you to visualize a team of people from different backgrounds that inspire you. Do the following exercise:

Create your Power Team. What I mean by this is imagine a team of people who inspire you; now visualize yourself as one or all of them in different scenarios, for instance, if you need to feel sexy, then have someone on your team who you feel is really sexy.

For example:

Sexy: Pamela Anderson, Marilyn Monroe, Eva Mendes (How would Pamela, Eva or Marilyn come across on a date?).

Confident: Alesha Dixon, Beyoncé, Reese Witherspoon, Susannah Reid, Holly Willoughby, Nicole Kidman, Anne Hathaway, Julia Roberts, Julie Walters, Emma Thompson.

Intelligent and Strong: Oprah Winfrey, Karen Brady, Sheryl Kara Sandberg, Dame Mary Berry, Deborah Meaden.

Funny and Confident: Jennifer Aniston, Amy Schumer, Barbara Streisand.

Who do you think is ultra-confident? I personally think Amanda Holden is a great example, or Cameron Diaz. Both are mature, gorgeous women who always present themselves well and know how to make an impact in every room they go into. Were they always like this? No, they had vulnerabilities when they were younger like everyone else.

Now ask yourself this: How would Amanda or Cameron make an entrance? Would these ladies hold their heads high, give direct eye contact, smile and walk with swagger? You know that they would, and you need to rehearse doing the same; practice until it becomes a habit.

I'm not saying change your personality, but just visualize yourself as someone like Amanda or Cameron. Tip: Think about your ideal role model for this exercise. Practice a few times with friends before you go out so you're feeling more confident. It may feel embarrassing at first, but you are better off stumbling in front of a best friend than your date.

Imagine the following scenario, you are meeting your date at a restaurant, before walking in you take a moment to get into character so you become in this example Amanda or Cameron you walk in with confidence, shoulders back, head held high, big smile. Partway through dinner you might be getting on really well and having a giggle so switch to Jennifer or Amy.

Try this exercise as it really works. The characters need to be people who you really admire so have fun and create your team.

Chapter 15: Ghosting and be an onion

"Be you as everyone else is already taken". - Oscar Wilde

Ghosting is sometimes a gradual process and sorry guys, but it is generally men and there is a reason for this I promise.

Here are some of the early signs:

- They struggle to make plans and especially long term.
- They certainly don't like to share too much personal information.
- They rarely respond to texts or calls and go missing for days with great excuses!
- Conversation lacks much emotion, depth and appears aloof.

A test to find out if they are into you and not ghosting you, is to get them to agree to book a trip and perhaps if you book it and they give you a deposit as that is showing some sort of commitment, but make sure you protect yourself so you are not out of pocket!

Ghosting can also occur on social media. On WhatsApp the person may block you for a few days or take down their social media so leaving you lost and confused and they know they are not able to make contact so they don't feel the shame.

Can you imagine if they were doing this you see them typing on WhatsApp and you have sent 3 or 4 messages especially when it's to check they are okay and honestly some people get off on this, but most will delete the app or block you leaving you are left feeling bloody frustrated.

Why do guys ghost you ? You see what guys are doing and it's in their DNA so they can't help it! Their main job is to make you fall in love with them. It's a bit like the Cavemen era the hunter gather, once they know they have you and you have fallen in love with them, it's only then they decided if they want to be with you long term and if they go off the radar don't chase them, ignore them and you will soon see them coming back for you! As they can't stand rejection.

Do you really want to date a waster? There are actually nice men out there.

When you are dating, put your barriers up for the first few months and don't be too available and don't give away too much, by all means let them know you, but not in depth and be like an onion peeling back your layers slowly. For a guy this is more intriguing and they will find you interesting and fascinating and want to know more.

Like the guy, keep it casual and don't be needy, make sure you have your time with your friends or for your hobbies and this is really good way to keep a healthy relationship, it's all about balance and if you fall into the trap off being full on, in time it will become claustrophobic, unhealthy and you will have certainly made a rod for your own back.

It's always best to start a relationship the way you mean to go on in your relationship, we all need time apart even when you're married and yes it is slightly difficult when you have kids but still make that "you time" as it's actually good for the both of you.

I have one rule, if you have been on a date text once and that's it! Example: Thank you for a great date. I had a really nice time. If he doesn't respond, DO NOT TEXT BACK.

You see if he or she wants you they will text you without fail. Sometimes things happen if he or she is in hospital then that's the only time to let them off but there is no excuse. It takes seconds to text even if it's an emoji. It shows they care and they are thinking about you, but if they don't text you then do not contact them as they are generally **not interested.**

I know it can be hard and maybe analyse why. What happened on the date, don't go all inspector Clouseau, but ask yourself did you feel anything went wrong and don't worry about nerves as those are normal, and certainly don't beat yourself up, learn from it and dust yourself down and go again, and remember to be the onion!

It can be so much fun on a first date and the next date could meet a lifelong friend or it could be your soul mate so you never know and it's really good practice.

It will also boost your confidence and after a few dates you will start to feel more and more confident and you might even learn lessons about yourself so it's really helpful to learn about yourself honestly that's why we are on this planet to learn lessons and go through all the emotions.

Have a great time and think about it no cooking! LOL

Chapter 16: Conversation for the first date

"Conversation is food for the soul" - Unknown

Even if you've been on 100 first dates, it's always nerve-wracking meeting someone for the first time or if you are starting to date a new beau. You don't want things to be awkward or the chatter to stall, you don't want to seem too nosey or overly curious, so how can you prepare to keep the conversation flowing? I've compiled a list of some of what I consider the best questions to ask on a first date.

Not only will these questions help you get to know your new acquaintance, but they'll also help guide you through a few deep conversations and help you keep things moving. Perhaps you don't need help when it comes to awkward situations on first dates, but for those of you who never know what to say, this is for you!

- **What's something you wish you could spend more time doing?**

This question will give you a better look at how they currently spend their time, why they're too busy to pursue their interests, and what their interests actually are. You'll also learn what they're passionate about and a few goals they have for the future, too.

- **What would your perfect vacation look like?**

This lighthearted topic will help you understand how they operate when it comes to adventure and travel. Do they prefer a margarita on the beach or do they like to trek through history-filled destinations, learning as much as possible along the way? You can find common ground and talk about where you've both already been and where you hope to go when life returns to "normal."

- **What was the highlight of your week?**

This question will give you a glimpse behind the scenes of their day-to-day life. Perhaps they'll tell you about something that happened at work, something that happened among their family or loved ones, or maybe they'll share more about a hobby they enjoy. You can chat more about the events that can really make a week feel special.

- **What are your friends like?**

This casual inquiry will tell you a lot about a man. You'll get to see what he thinks of his friends, how he values their friendship, and whether or not he is in touch with his sensitive side. As they say, you are who you spend time with! Pay attention to the kinds of friends this person keeps around as it will certainly help you understand what they're like, as well.

Chapter 17: Why does a relationship fail? Why is jam so important in your relationship!

"Be there for others, but never leave yourself empty".- Lisa Holley Palmer

This is a big question with many answers and it's difficult unless you are in front of me! To generalise, I am going to give you some guidance.

The 4 main reasons why a relationship fails:

- **Trust**
- **Communication**
- **Respect**
- **Intimacy**

TRUST – The number one reason always comes down to trust. It's so important to feel secure in a relationship as it's just a ticking time bomb. When your partner is vague, unreliable and makes you feel insecure and that you're not one of the most important people in their life, as you need to feel secure! and if your partner has lied to you.

A little white lie like, if a woman has been shopping, let's face it we all hide the bags in the boot LOL but this is ok or I am on my way home babe and you know full well they are stopping off for a pint, well that's sort of ok too, but if he or she is on the missing list for hours and hours and always turning their phone off and hiding their phone this is the start to make you feel insecure and the cracks will appear.

Personally, I feel we know deep down something's not quite right. Again you don't want to come overly possessive as there is truly nothing worse than watching over a partner all the time as you feel like life is being sucked out of you and this is so unhealthy in a relationship, it's all about balance and trusting your partner.

RESPECT – is a huge component in a relationship and not taking anyone for granted, it broke so many relationships during Covid as a lot of couples were working from home and managing the kids, dinner, cleaning and it's about respecting your partner and not expecting from your partner! So just because he's the man he should mow the lawn or the woman needs to cook every night, it's the 21st Century!

Respect does come to honouring your partner and mirroring what you put out you get back. So perhaps if your partner takes out the bins do it for them or if your partner always cooks surprise them when they get in! Even if it is beans on toast just add a bit of green garnish or put the beans in a heart shape, and hey presto! It's all about the little gestures.

One of the **BIGGEST** issues comes down to money, this is tough as a lot of people are really struggling with the cost of fuel and living, don't get me started haha! You often find in a relationship one partner takes control of the finances which is fine. As long as you respect your partner and treat them as your partner when it comes to money and DO NOT treat them like your superior and you have the right to spend more than them as this is just going to cause arguments.

The best way to stop conflict is to have a spreadsheet and write down what comes in and what goes out and how much you have left. Then sitting down and discussing in an adult manner. This truly does stop the arguments and gives you both total respect for each other.

COMMUNICATION – I know I don't stop talking about communication, but this is one of the killers in a relationship! You see it's great at the start of a relationship the fun, excitement, the friends, holidays, the sex.

Then comes along the kids, the mortgage, and responsibilities… yawn! Then your life is all about the kids, household chores and money! It comes back to balance and having a healthy balance in your life.

It's very important to have your own life outside of your relationship, and hobbies as this is so healthy but also gives you time apart and something to talk about.

You definitely need a date night, and there should be at least once a month if not 2 or 3 times a month depending on budgets! It doesn't have to cost a lot showing you care and having fun.

INTIMACY – I get it you have been at work all day come home and you're bloody knackered! All you want to do is sit down with the TV or have a hot relaxing bath. Who has that time? LOL!

Well, we need to make time for our mental health as it is so important having a little time out for yourself, and relaxing is important as when you feel relaxed and comfortable, you will be more inclined to have sex. I think if your husband or wife has been at work all day, find out when they are on their way home and run a nice bath, put some candles out as men love these too, I know they might not show it but they secretly do and include some nice bubble bath. Sharing is caring!

When you make time for your partner and make them feel loved and appreciated, most people want to please their partner as it's the little things they have done to make them feel loved and appreciated.

I do see a lot of couples talk about sex and it's the same old, I'm tired… well spice it up a bit! If your partner is a morning person why not make them laugh, put some honey or jam on your bits and tell them breakfast is ready, it will make them laugh and bring some fun back into the relationship.

I do have a fun product on my website which will certainly make your eyes water and give you both a right laugh! More details at the end.

Guys come on, what do women love? Chocolate… well I am sure I don't have to tell you what to do with that! Bringing back fun and laughter is so important! Wind each other up with text messages, make them saucy, and cheeky as a way to a woman's heart is a funny, confident man!

Guys, women need to feel loved so go and give them a cuddle and a bottle of bubbles, LOL, then you will certainly have a good night! Let's hope she doesn't fall asleep hehe!

Just remember **BALANCE** is key, have fun and get the jam out!

Chapter 18: Attracting the right person

"Always believe something wonderful is around the corner, because it is" - Lisa Holley Palmer.

I am going to demonstrate in some images about our development from a child to an adult and how much our attraction and vibration can change over time. There are also a few real life stories used for illustration purposes but their names are changed and with their permission.

How can we attract the right person, but first as I have said in previous chapters it all starts with you and you being the best version of yourself.

If you take **Image A**

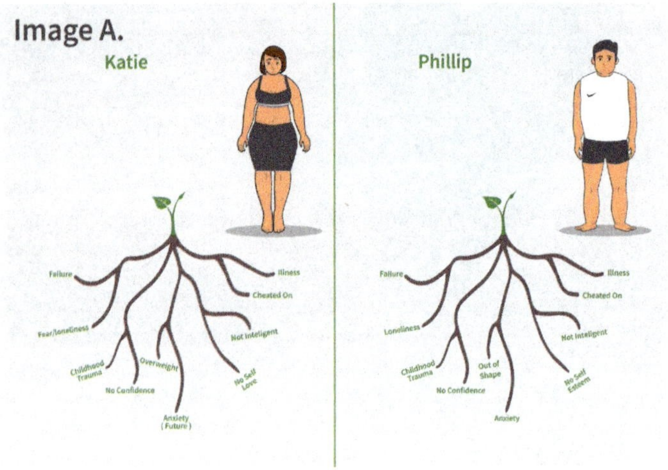

We have Katie in image A.

Katie’s underlying issues her core beliefs:
She has all these emotions:
Failure
Fear of being lonely

Childhood trauma
Overweight
No confidence
Anxiety about the future
No self love
Not intelligent
Cheated on
Underlying Illness.

Then we look at Phillip also in image A
He's core beliefs:
Failure
Lonely
Childhood trauma
No confidence
Out of shape
Anxiety
No self esteem
Not Intelligent
Cheated on
Underline illness

Katie has a lot of emotions, fears and underlying issues that she never dealt with and you see under the line are the issues and above the line is the seed of growth and as you can see Katie has not developed much.

She feels she is not intelligent, she probably is intelligent but if she feels that way then that's going to be affecting her emotionally.

You see in the image A - Katie is vibrating and energetically attracting a similar vibration to her, guess what, she ends up dating Phillip also in image A and he is also vibrating at the same frequency although his emotions are slightly different he is exactly the same.

Image B

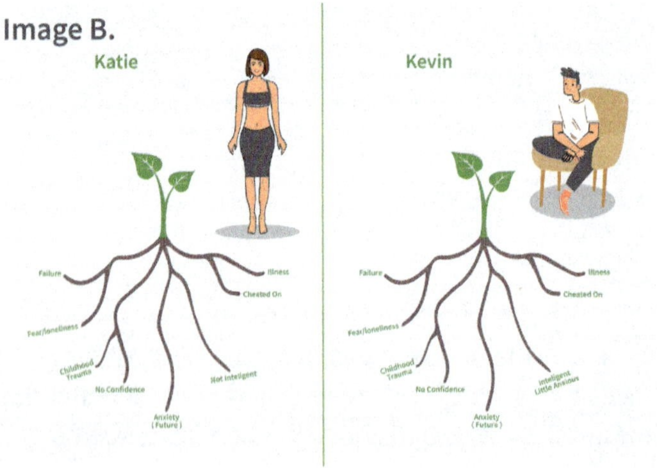

Katie has decided to take some action, she has decided to start going to the gym and looking after herself, so Katie has made a plan to visit the gym 4 times a week. Guess what happens over time? Yes you guessed right, she is starting to lose weight and feel more confident in her weight.

The relationship fizzles out with Phillip and Katie then starts to look for another relationship as she is feeling great about her appearance.

She attracts Kevin and let's look at Kevin aka Mr Sobsad in Image B.

Katie as you can see she has worked on appearance and losing weight if you see these emotions below the line they have gone!

See across on Image B who has she attracted? Kevin Sobsad.

Who is Mr Sobsad? He sits on his backside all day.

Why has she chosen someone like this? As Katie is a bit of a workaholic she's not lazy she is starting to feel better about herself which is fantastic, but she still feels deep down she is not good enough as one of her core beliefs.

Here is the big BUT she still has lots of underlying issues. Why did she attract Mr Sobsad?
He is lazy, but why is he lazy? He hides his emotions and attracts someone who is active as he sends out wrong vibrations and disguises who he is and shows up vibrationally that he is super confident, active, hardworking and the life and soul of the party.

He was larger than life and the loudest person at the party so you can see why she is attracted to him as she just loved his confidence.

Deep down and hidden, guess what? When you get to know Kevin Sobsad he doesn't feel good enough, this is a deep rooted core belief, so on the outside he is showing he's confident but deep down he's not and has a lot of underlying issues similar to Katie.

Overtime Katie has started to grow and the problem was Mr Sobsad didn't grow he became jealous and resentful, Katie was getting more confident and going out, Mr Sobsad would stay in, He was invited to go out but he declined and then he wouldn't talk to Katie when she came in as he was jealous.

Lets see in Image C what Katie did to see why Katie and Mr Sobsad partied ways:

Image C

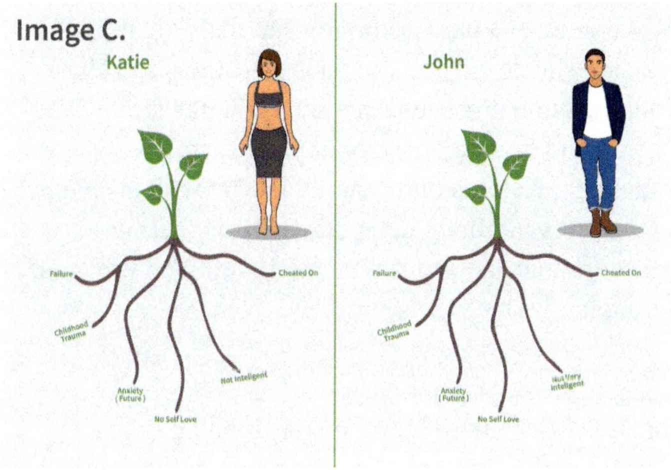

Image C - Katie decided she would start looking at nutrition and eating healthier as she was always ill and felt tired and it used to make her feel slightly down.

Katie worked on eating healthy, having a balanced diet and she had lost weight but what was happening was she was getting really toned. So her underlying illness has now gone and guess what else has gone?

her fear of loneliness as she was getting a lot of male attention as she looked great on the outside.

Katie goes to a party although she feels great on the outside she doesn't on the inside. At the party she looks around and sees this guy. He looks smiley and happy and he's quiet. They have the same body language, Katie is putting on a face that she is happy and smiley although deep down she is feeling insecure that she is not very intelligent and not good enough.

Image C Lets meet John, look at John he's very similar and guess what he's vibrating at the same frequency.

John looked happy at the party he came across confident but deep down he is also insecure.

Why? If we look deeper, he was bullied as a kid. He grew up on a council estate. His core belief is he is not good enough.

Katie suffered from dyslexia and at school felt she was not intelligent, the children at the school called her names and they are still rooted in her core beliefs that she is not good enough.
John has similar issues to not feeling good enough as his core belief.

This is ok as long as they both work together on these issues. Sometimes you don’t realise you have these issues, until you meet someone or start looking at why things have happened.

A really good question to ask yourself and journal is “Why do I feel like this” and keep asking yourself and journaling until you have the answer. It might take you an hour or so but we have the answer within.

Most relationships (family, boyfriend, friend, work colleague, husband) will show you what's lacking or what issues you haven't dealt with.

Image D

Let's look at Image D, Katie has been working on her childhood trauma and also she has been cheated on in the past. This has not helped with her core belief of not feeling good enough.

This took a little time, Katie has developed more and more self belief and self love.

Guess what happened to John? He saw how much Katie was growing as a person and he helped her grow and encouraged her to grow.

Katie was getting some coaching and guess what happened? John decided to do the same as he loved how much Katie was more confident and he could see how much she was growing as a person and he loved to see her happy so he decided to do the same.

Image E

Let’s look at Image E. What did Katie and John do?

They went on lots of training courses that they were both interested in. They would read a lot more and guess what happened. They both felt they were more intelligent and they started to travel more which gave them even more intelligence and culture. John started to feel more self worth as he was becoming more confident and intelligent.

You see it won't happen overnight, but if you can be the best version of yourself. You're going to feel so good about yourself and yes we are all going to have little niggles.
We are human after all, but we won't fully get rid of anxiety as no one can ever control the future.

What you can do is do everything you can to be the best you! And having a supportive partner will change your life, if you don't have a supportive partner work on yourself and be the best of you and see how much prouder, stronger and progress you make.

When I go back to some of the previous chapters, relationships are great and they teach us a lot about ourselves.

It is also good to find a relationship when you have dealt with some of your underlying root causes and feel on top of the world.

So please learn from each relationship and look at what caused the breakdown/breakup and work on it until you feel better about the situation and yourself.

Chapter 19: Which men to avoid and who to marry!

"You don't marry the person you can live with - you marry the person you can't live without" - Unknown

I have interviewed thousands of men and women from all over the world for my job, I have certainly met some incredibly interesting people over the years and there have certainly been some people I have not taken on or avoided like the plague.

Let me introduce you to the 9 types of men:

Mr Alyd - Always lets you down

Mr Alyd is a little bit sensitive and self-absorbed. He doesn't mean to be, it's just his DNA.

He has highs and lows. One minute he is on a high and happy and looking forward to meeting up and making plans.

Then the next day is low and doesn't feel like going out or meeting up and wants solidarity.

When he's up he's up and really talkative and fun to be around, yes you guessed it when he's on a low he's not great to be around and it's best if he has his own space to work things out, he's very sensitive at this time and will easily be offended if you said something and will go into his shell.

If he is at a party when he is on a high and that's the only time you will generally see him, he will be very self-centred and won't tend to ask you questions it's all about him and his life and his problems.

He can be very funny and make you laugh it's a bit like dating a rollercoaster you get the amazing highs and what goes up must go down. He tends to a nice person, he's kind but he can get quite low and its best to show support but let him have his man time. Go out with the girls and have fun!

Mr Sobsad - Sits on back side all day.

Mr Sobsad, he tends to portray an air of confidence and will use their body weight to dominate a social gathering by being overpowering, giving off the image of life and soul of the party.

At the party he will only stick with people he is close to; he will generally not start a conversation with others as he will wait for them to talk to him unless there is something in it for him.

Deep down they are often insecure and not motivated and lazy. They like their partner to be active, so they make up for their lazy life ethic.

They don't generally like an outgoing partner as he won't be able to dominate her. He likes to have his friends and family close by to give him his boost of greatness.

If you are expecting great sex, you'll be lucky; better go and treat yourself to a nice rabbit and I am not on about the fluffy type wink wink!

Mr Hnse - Have no self-esteem

This guy is totally charming, generally handsome, dresses well and gives you flutters when you look at him. You know the type right? He has a reasonably good job, he has the patter he could talk his way out of anything. He's exciting, smart, you just fall for his charm. He will use material assets to charm you.

If this guy is married he will generally never leave his wife, and the affairs never translate into anything meaningful for him to leave his wife.

You will probably not know he has a partner at the beginning, until he knows he has you hook line and sinker.

He will make every excuse under the sun and have a great story about why he can't leave his wife.

Bless his poor wife. Some women don't know for a long time and then wise up, please listen to your instincts if you are married to this one.

I know he will turn the charm right up and make you feel you are the only one and treat you so well.

He will never stop cheating. He can't help it. He might go for a year or few years but 99% will cheat again and they can't help it. If you are the wife reading this please love yourself enough to find the right man who deserves you.

You see he needs it to boost his self esteem.

He will not feel much emotion for the other women he is cheating with and there is a good chance he may have a few women.

This guy generally has a high libido. He just sees the affair as a reward for his charming personality and way to prove to himself that he has still got it.

I’m afraid most Mr HNSE won't change it is just in their DNA.

Mr Hiaw - He is always working. Aka Piers Morgan

Mr Hiaw is very hardworking, very intelligent and has such a great work ethic and tends to be a provider and will put his family at the top of his priority.

He does love attention and knows exactly how to get it and will come across as authoritative figure and will command an audience, he is very assertive and leader in his field.

He is a great father but will always have an opinion on most things and will dominate most of his family and social gatherings, but not in a narcissistic way but just he likes to be heard, but why not, he is pretty cool and is a great conversationalist.

He has great values and morals. Mr Hiaw will support you and give you encouragement, this relationship will be meeting of the minds.

My opinion if your happy his voice will be heard the loudest and you will have to go where he tends to enjoy but that will be amazing as he likes the finer things in life, then you won't go wrong as he will take great care of you and the family, he tends to be a one-woman man.

Marry this one!

Mr Cyem - Control your every move.

Mr Cyem tends to be in the gym when he's young and will always worry about his appearance, will never show it.

They will come across confident and outgoing but actually they tend to be very insecure. They don't like social gatherings unless it's their friends or family.

He will want to control your every move, they tend to like someone polar opposite, someone who's bubbly and outgoing, attractive, he will try and break you and control your every move, it's actually quite draining being with Mr Cyem. He is very good at making you feel on top of the world one minute, then down the next because of his constant moods and control.

The highs are high and lows are very low, its like a roller coaster. Its hard to break the cycle, its like a loop and your caving the highs, you will always be walking on egg shells. Most relationships have a small up and downs but this will be quite extreme.

He is generally very negative person will drain your energy.

When he knows your fed up with him again, he turns on the charm full blast and he will lead you into a full sense of security.

Money will play a big part in his control over you, that's why it's always best to have a separate bank account and that goes for any relationship. Always have your own money and bank account, it’s ok to have a joint one but don't let any relationship control your private one.

I would run for the hills and hide from him!

Mr Icsn - I can't say no

Mr Iscn is what we call the teddy bear. He works as hard as he has to but will generally not work weekends because he doesn't want to overdo it.

He's a very kind and caring man and his family mean everything to him.

He will love you unconditionally and will provide but he will never be wealthy, but you will know where you are with him.

He tends to not be controlling and if you were out with your friends, he would be the first one to pick you all up. He makes a great father figure; he would be the type to read a story to your children and give them a bath and nurture, he’s a great family man.

He's the type of guy everyone loves as he will always be there for everyone and that's normally the problem, he can't say NO.

He will show you great strength if you have a problem, he will be there for you and back you all the way.

He would give you his last dollar, so watch out as he is a big cuddly teddy bear but if you're looking for someone with leadership skills, he's not your man but one of my favourites overall as you will be able to trust this beautiful kind man, but you will never be rich but you will be in rich in his wonderful qualities and that's gold in my books.

He likes to go to football/sport that doesn’t take to much effort so he can relax, he can show his emotion as a lot of men struggle to show their emotions and that's why a lot of men like sport, so they can let out their emotions (let them go its good for men, plus you can watch what you want on the box LOL)

Its particularly important for Mr Icsn as he struggles with his emotions and its good for him to have this time to release them or if he has the game on at home let him have this time as he will really enjoy himself.

This guy is a real treasure, marriage material!

Mr Foch - Frightened of commitment himself

Mr Foch is generally very intelligent and analytical; he tends to be a CEO or will be part of the executive team and generally in technology. He will like responsibility in his work life as he can control this. He is very independent and ambitious.

He tends to like the finer things in life, but he is quite happy in his own company. If he ever does decide to commit and that will generally take a long time. If he does start dating you, then he will give you his all.

He likes deep meaningful relationships. But he will like his own space to think as thinking time is a very important part of who he is. If you need attention all the time, he is not the guy for you.

He knows exactly what he wants, and he generally always gets what he wants, you tend to find it his way or the highway, but he will have already made his mind up if he lets you in and that's why he takes so long on commitment as he needs to be 110%.

He can be slightly manipulative and persuasive. He generally likes a sense of adventure and travel will be an important part of his DNA.

Mr Icda - I can do anything!

He is a good man with very strong values, he is the caveman and very narrow minded. It's not his fault it's the way he was brought up.

He lives in a world where does not see outside of the box, when it comes to your career he will see things very black and white and will not support you if its not a practical job.

He will have had a very difficult relationship mother and not had much love or nurturing.

He really struggles to show any emotion as he has bottled it up most of his life, as in his mind emotion is weakness. I like to call this man Superman as he will support you financially and fix anything rather than pay someone to do it and when the chips are down he will always get the money to put food on the table for his family.

He will never ask for help, he's a worker, and he would do anything for anyone but don't underestimate him he's very astute and a very clever man.

He will tend to be well off. As his head is down working and grafting that's all his life is truly about.

I'm afraid if you're looking for a loving deep connection, talking relationship from this man you are not going to get it. If you're a needy person you will struggle in the relationship as this relationship will not be touchy, feely.

If you are happy doing your own thing then he will be a good provider for you.

His way of showing you love is working and providing, he will always put a roof over your head and food on the table.

He's clever and generally good with his hands he can fix and mend anything. Mr Icda loves his own space and you will generally find him in his man cave.

He is looking for someone who is solid, grounded, reliable and practical.

He can't deal with drama, but he will expect his dinner on the table with a clean and tidy house, he is very set in his ways! You are not going to be able to change him STUBBORN!

Mr Atku - Anything to keep you

Mr Atku The manipulator will do anything to keep you and do anything to be able to get what he wants, so that could be drink, drugs it's all to do with addiction and he knows how to keep you and how to play the game, this is whole purpose in life because he hasn't dealt with his issues and a lot of them are from his childhood or past life he will destroy you and I'm going to add a story on here and this relates to all addictions.

You need to take back your power; you can only lead a horse to water.

You will tend to find Mr Atku will threaten to hurt himself or destroy you if you leave and to have the power over you so just be careful and talk to a specialist and keep all the evidence as a word of warning.

Get on a plane, hide and don't come out until he's gone!

ALCOHOLISM - I wanted to write this so you can completely understand an alcoholic and understand the way they are. Just so you know, I am not alcoholic, I only have one and I'm tiddly.

Consider yourself warned; brutal honesty lies ahead. In fact, I can't avoid brutal honesty, because as an alcoholic, nothing matters except for my next drink - not even the truth.

I am an alcoholic. Not your friend, not your partner, not your parent or your child. That person is gone, having only left behind the idea and memory of whoever I once was to you.

In fact, it's impossible for me to care about anything *other* than alcohol. I can't even care about you. The only thing I can manage to care about - or look forward to - is my next drink.

It's not a want, it's a need, and I'll go through you to make sure my needs are met.

The reality is that when I look at you, all I see is opportunity. But not an opportunity for love or support…an opportunity to manipulate my way to my next sweet, intoxicating sip.

It doesn't matter who you are to me. It doesn't matter what you need. So long as you have money, I'll keep you in my life - but only at an arm's length, of course. Because if you have money, you are valuable to me. It doesn't matter if you have bills to pay, it doesn't matter if you're hungry, or sick, or poor. As long as you have enough for me to steal or sell, you are still useful to me...for now.

And so…I'll lurk in the background. I'll wait until your walls are down, or until you are not looking. I will take what *you* have to get what *I* need. And I simply don't care how that makes you feel.

While you might think you can love me hard enough to change me, or support me long enough to save me, but you simply could not be more wrong. You see, your love no longer matters to me. I don't care if you're upset, sad, angry, or disappointed, though I might lie and tell you I do in order to get my hands on your last dollar.

My value system is compromised, and my morals have flown out the window. It doesn't matter what I have to say or do, I'll say and do whatever in order to get my next sip. I'll continue to lie, cheat, and steal from you in order to feed the monster in me. The monster that craves alcohol and chaos. I'm no longer me, I'm just the monster. And the monster doesn't care if your heart gets broken.

Strangely…you might grow to be fond of the monster inside me. Because you know that when the monster gets hungry, you - and your wallet - have my attention, my facade of love. But once you've given into the monster, and I've gotten what I need, I'll turn my back on you once again to drink, drink, drink myself away. You'll continue to reach out…to check on me…to offer your help to me. And the monster will happily accept.

You see, by supporting me, you help keep me sick and imprisoned by the monster. You might believe that you're supporting me, making a positive impact on my life, but what you're really doing is tightening the grip that alcohol has on me.

This dance we do…it'll lead us to death. My body - and mind - will betray me, or you'll be left without a penny to your name, broken hearted and stressed to death. I'll shrug it off like it's nothing. We can blame the monster…we can blame the alcohol.

I hope that helped you understand an addict and honestly be very careful as they are very clever!

A functioning alcoholic is the worst as they can disguise it so well and have a break for a few weeks making you believe they are not an alcoholic but they are, so be very careful!

With all those 9 types of men which I am sure you have probably come across some or maybe all of them. Please do try to forgive those who didn't know how to love you. They were teaching you how to love yourself.

Chapter 20 - How to communicate with the five different types of communication styles.

"An exceptional relationship starts with great conversation" - Lisa Holley Palmer

How to communicate? There are five different types of communication styles and you need to understand how to communicate with your partner so you are understood and how to win the battle.

Knowing how to communicate with the five different types will help you in any situation if that's at work, family, or a loved one or even if you're selling or pitching an idea. You need to understand what makes that person tick and how they listen to you.

The art of communication:

Mr Analytical

You have the analytical communicator and they are very direct and sometimes you feel they are not warm as they are so direct but that is untrue, it's the way they communicate and think. They rely on solid facts and data and they will totally avoid any emotional validation when talking, you might feel they are making cold rational decisions without emotion.

They are very articulate and logical and you tend to feel they have no feelings, but these are hidden when communicating as they tend to be deep in thought when they talk.

If you are having an argument or an in depth discussion make sure you have your facts and show them both sides of the argument. It's always best to give them time to think things through with no pressure. You can't take it personally when they discuss things with you in a cold manner; it's just in their DNA.

Mr Intuitive

These guys are completely visual. They see images in their mind so when they are in discussion you will see them as if they are looking at an image in their minds-eye.

When communicating with Mr. Intuitive, it's good to create a picture in your mind so you can explain in such a way they will get it. It's always good to give lots of detail, as if they can see it they can build it, but if they don't understand or can't see it they just don't get it, they can become frustrated and bored and will switch off, it's totally important to engage them with the big picture.

If you are in a heated argument Mr. Intuitive, he will feel highly uncomfortable if he doesn't understand the bigger picture, remembering plenty of detail will help eliminate those kinds of problems.

Example if this was a work colleague it would be really good to show them in visual images or like a storyboard as it will completely click with them and they will fully understand you.

Mr Functional

Mr Functional in my words wants to know the ins and outs of a duck's backside excuse the duck lol They love a step by step guide. It's a bit like giving them an Ikea flat pack and instructions and they are happy as they have a road map with full instructions to follow (drives me mad the bloody Ikea flat back, it generally goes in the bin LOL)

They like organisation and structure, you must know the type as we all have that friend who you go on holiday with and out come's the itinerary up 7.05am, breakfast at 7.35am and out for a walk. 8.15am and then shower, you got it love 'em or hate them at least you know where you are with this type and you probably have the schedule where they are LOL.

If this was a work example you need to have details, plan an in depth process to follow from start to finish timelines and milestones so they know exactly where they are.

If you are in a argument they are practical and it's always best to have a true purpose for this argument and set your own timeline yourself so you have something booked later that day so you know you have a time when this argument will be over and you can make up, as Mr Functional will deep down know he needs to finish this argument at a set time as he has a schedule to complete. Thank me later!

Mr Personal

Ahh these are the emotional ones, they lead with their emotions and feelings in everything they do.

Mr Personal tends to be very approachable and good listeners and great advisors as they can feel how someone is feeling. They truly value someone who has plenty of thought and feeling. If you're in a bad mood they tend to feel that and will tend to mirror how you're feeling so it's best if you want to be happy and fake it baby! Be happy or give yourself an affirmation “When I feel happy I manifest more reasons to be happy”.

If you have a problem they are great to resolve conflict and will tend to have your back as conflict is their strength, they will weigh in on different perspectives.

If you're having an argument try not to upset him as they are going to be very emotional “emtoballs” your probably end up feeling bad as you will tend to see how upset they are as they are great at showing their emotions, so it's best to sit down have a grown up convo and keep it positive as he will mirror you and how you are feeling and come across.

Mr Passive

The passive type tends to fail at expressing their feelings and have trouble explaining in depth. They know what they want to say but find it difficult to express their words leaving them feeling frustrated and sometimes angry.

If they are in an argument they tend to be quiet and hide in their shell as they hate confrontation.

They tend to lack posture and eye contact due to the fact they are not feeling great about communication themselves because they are frustrated and they tend to go with the flow, as they would rather have peace.

If you're in an argument it is better to talk slowly, never be aggressive or shout as they will turn inward and you will get nothing from them and they will cause friction and problems down the road. It's better to have a meaningful conversation and a quiet conversation and let them think and don't expect an answer, you need to give them time.

These people are happy go-lucky and just want complete peace in their life. It's better to talk about how you feel to them and let them communicate back to you when they are ready, it's always best if you're dating someone like this to have quality time together so they feel loved and appreciated.

Chapter 21 - Out with the old and in with the new.

"*What is imminent is better than what is gone" - Lisa Holley Palmer*

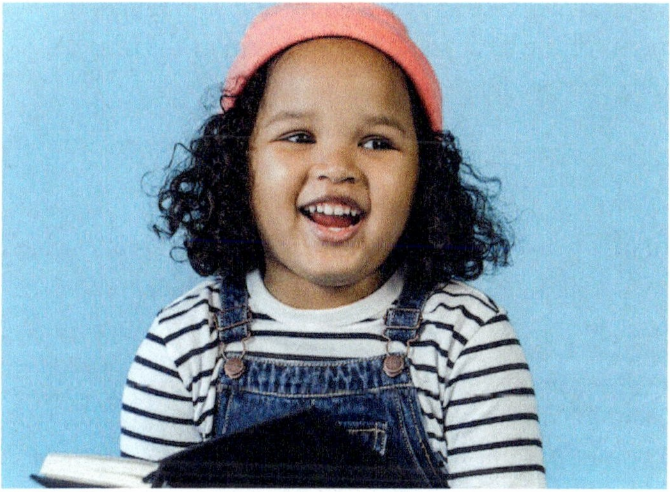

How do we move forward? It's a good question as you need to be ready to move forward, but you can't if you're living in the past.

The art of letting go! You see we hold on so tight to everything out of fear, that could be a relationship as we are scared to be on our own, but to make room for good you have to let go of what is not serving you! I want to tell you a couple of stories.

A friend of mine's mum passed away and deeply missed her and felt lonely without her. She held onto all her stuff, all her clothes, shoes, and sideboard literally she had everything but the kitchen sink LOL. Anyway, I spoke to her one day and said to make room for the new you have to get rid of the old, it's your fear holding you back.

I explained you have your mum's memories and what good is it doing hauling all this stuff! She agreed it was getting in the way and cluttering her home.

I said give it to charity or sell it and buy a nice tree in memory of your mum. She did that over the course of the week. Then the last day when she got rid of it all she met this lady in the charity shop.

It turns out this lady used to know her mum and they were great friends from school and they arranged to meet for lunch the following week.

This lady hasn't replaced her mum, but it moved the stale energy and brought her a gift.

You see the universe will replace what has gone and this lady has helped my friend move on and feel she is close to her mum again which is so lovely.

I also have another short story and I want you to do this so over the course of the next 7 days. I want you to throw out 21 items a day and that could be a pair of old knickers or those jeans you have kept for 10 years holding on to just in case you can't fit back into them or old pills, to maybe an old engagement ring from an ex.

You see you're telling the universe I don't need these and I will be well and won't have this problem again and throw them out or sell them.

I did this on the second day I threw out an old pad it had lots of notes and it was a pain as I didn't have a notepad but it was old stuff in it that I didn't really need, some of the written stuff was from the past and I also threw out pack 4 highlighters as they worked but wasn't great, they had old memories attached to them as someone who wasn't a good person had used them.

I bet like me you have lots of old items etc we just hold on to. So I threw them out and I swear on my life my son came home from work that night. I hadn't told him what I had been doing.

He came into my room and said mum got something for you as he is moving jobs in the same company and didn't need it. He gave me a new pad and a blue highlighter.

You see if you have to lose your car or a job or partner it's not easy, but you will have a replacement and it might not happen straight away but it will be replaced. You just need to give the universe time to catch up and trust it will happen and bring you better things in your life.

So I want you to go through your things, draws and cupboards over the course of the next 7 days and remove 21 items a day, I can guarantee you this you will feel a sense of achievement, and accomplishment and you will see things start to change! So out with the old and in with the new.

Next and this is a very important part of life, I know I talk about it lots but BALANCE is truly the key in everything we do in life!

I have added below an image of life and everything we have in life.

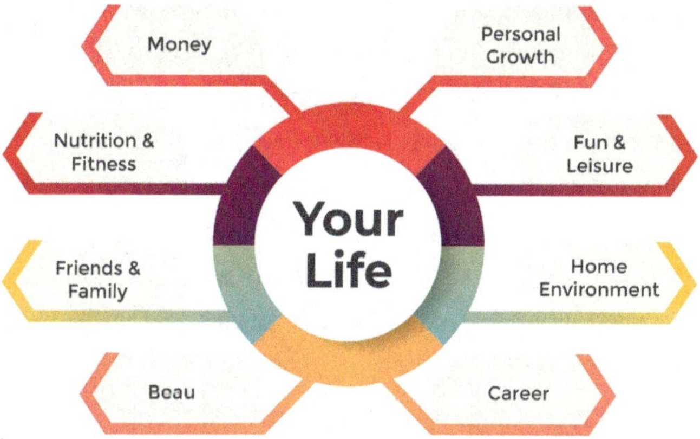

Lisa Holley Palmer

Next, I want you to print this image and review every part of your life. If you can't go to www.mogullove.com for the free download.

Next, I want you to write the first number that pops into your head, for example, let's go with fun and leisure and out of 1 to 10 and 10 being strong you put the number you feel relates to that part of your life. Example 3 and this will demonstrate where you are putting energy into what section of your life and those parts you are not giving enough attention to.

I hope this demonstrates to you that what needs to be worked at and if you look at Personal Growth that could be learning self-development or spiritual learning, reading more books or going on courses and remember knowledge is power and this will help you in other parts of life too.

I feel this is the year to look inward and to become more critical and analytical in finding **your**self…

I want to tell you another short story, this lady on her life chart, the only part of her life that was a 10 was work and money and the rest were pretty much 2 or 3 which is so unhealthy.

She didn't do anything about it until life caught up with her. You see it will turn up and bite you on the arse.

It did exactly that to this lady.

I love this quote "If you do not make time for your wellness, you will be forced to make time for your illness."

READ THAT AGAIN!

Please reevaluate everything in your life and balance it out before it balances you out!

From today, I want you to take a photo everyday of something that made you smile and journal about it and how it made you feel.

Some days you will have to look a little harder. Perhaps you could take a picture of a beautiful flower, perhaps it was a nice food that you had or perhaps it's a picture of your dog.

Animals can be so rewarding and very funny. I took my dog to the park and she went into the woods and came out with a pair of knickers. I tried to get her to drop them and she decided to run around the park with these knickers and everyone was watching me chase her the little sod! One chap said nice knickers LOL.

That picture and memory is one I will treasure. It's the little things and the more you do this taking pictures your subconscious mind is looking for more and more positive things in your everyday life.

Being grateful can have a positive impact on your life. It can improve mental and physical well-being, increase resilience, and foster better relationships.

Additionally, gratitude can help to shift your focus from negative thoughts and experiences to positive ones, leading to a more optimistic outlook and greater overall satisfaction with life.

Lastly, one of the most important questions:

So what does the perfect relationship look like?

First it starts with you. And you having a healthy happy loving relationship with you. If you go back to chapter 18 with Katie, see how much she changed and grew as a person so do it for you.

A good healthy happy relationship should be built on trust, honesty, respect and open dialog and your partner wanting you to grow, just like John did in chapter 18. He was supportive of Katie and they grew together.

A partner should always respect your independence and there is no imbalance of power, learn and grow together. We can compromise as long as it's done with the right intention and both parties are happy. He should be treating you like a Princess and that needs to be reciprocated.

Remember life is not a dress rehearsal we have one life so make it a good one!

I hope you enjoyed my book and I truly appreciate it if you could spare less than minute and give me a review on Amazon. Please tell your friends about the book so they don't have to go through a terrible relationship. Thank you so much.

I hope this book has given you all the tools to have a successful, happy, healthy relationship with yourself and others.

We have learnt how to know if someone is lying to you, and how to have a successful relationship. I hope if you are in a relationship or when you start dating dating you take up my "Alpha Dating" which I know your going to enjoy.

Don't forget the jam and make sure you totally avoid Mr Atku.

I hope you have lots of wonderful relationships with your beau, family, colleagues and understand how they communicate. Remember out with the old and in with the new and you certainly will feel cleansed.

Be sure you revaluate every part of your life and that you are giving your energy to the 8 different sections so you have balance and peace in your life.

If you have been in a relationship and sometimes you still feel attached and energetically connected to that ex.

If you head to www.snogmarryandhide.com I have added a few complimentary download's.

There is a video to release an ex and set yourself FREE!

I have ***created a free support group*** *for women of all ages. You will also find lots of useful thing like how to change your oil on the car, to how to put up a shelf, or cook along with me and Rustie Lee to dancing club, book club, singing club, you never need to feel alone.*

Plus we have over 32 global experts to help from financiers, lawyers, child psychologists, stylists, life coaches, beauty experts to fun things, like celebrity bingo. ***www.mogullove.com.*** *This site will be moved to www.mindjump.com check both just incase.*

If you would like to become a global matchmaker and a relationship coach with our accredited full training course. For more details head to mmib.club and sign up.

"Stay away from negative people. They have a problem for every solution." - Albert Einstein

Life is like a book; one chapter is happy, and one is sad, but if you don't turn the page, you never know what the next chapter holds.

Remember, when you meet the one, you could end up with him for the next forty years or more, so what are you waiting for? Go and have fun and choice wisely!

Trust that you are right where you need to be.

Lots of Love Lisa xx

Don't forget to follow me Instagram
@mslisaholleypalmer

You tube channel giving you lots of dating advice
@snogmarryandhide

Please follow on Instagram @pinkribbonfoundation please see more information below about this wonderful foundation.

With special thanks to

Illustrations by Jon Trafford

Pexels Images

Alex Green
Jill Wellington
Radu Florin
Monstera
Amina Wilkins
Bess Hamiti
Juan Vargas
Uzunov Rostislav

Anna Shvets
Ivan Babydov
Luis Quintero
Mike Van Schoonderwalt
Enes Turkoglu
Monstera
Ronda Productions
Yan Krukov
Ron Lach
Torsten Dettlaff
Rocketmann Team
Ivan Samkov
Markus Spiske
Gabriel Frank
Mikhal Nilov
Asad photo Maldives
Maverazehra Coskun
Gelatin
Alito Sunawang
Vera arsic
Zexy zw
Aliko-Sunawan
Designecologist
Cottonbro studio
Tima Miroschnichenko
Gary Whyte
Andrea Piacquadio

Pixabay Images

Kreingkral Luangchaipreeda
Stefan Keller
bravor1X
Sobima

Unsplash Images

Jamie Street
Tim Mossholder

Dr Arthur Cassidy thank you for all your support.

Darren Stanton Human Lie Detector
Thanks Darren for all you support very much appreciated.

Patricia Whitson aka my fairy god mother for all your help guidance and support I couldn't have done it without you.

To my beautiful son Bradley you truly have been an incredible son, I am the luckiest mum in the world you have the kindest soul inside and out.

To my lovely mum and dad I know I drive you up the wall at times and its not been easy! I am truly grateful for all your help and support and I am the luckiest daughter in the world to have you as my parents.

RIP To my fun loving kind Aunt Barbara you always made me laugh with your funny incredible champagne swigging lifestyle and your big warm heart.

To Mark T for your help and understanding and support I truly appreciate it and thank you for your friendship.

To Sue and Clive thank you so much for believing in me and all your support you truly have been a good friend.

To June and Mr Moosey, Colin Moose, Thank you for all your support and kindness over the years! Love you lots love Miss Moosey.

Anna Bruning thank you so much for the great advice lots of love, love you.

Lucinda Ellery for believing in me at the start and your support I will never forget it.

Jonathan Cooper love you and making me laugh crazy one.

Rustie Lee thank you for all your help and being a great friend love you lots.

I would like to thank Sandro Forte, Peter Dunne and Marion Farrelly for your continued support and love. Love you all Superstars.

Some of the proceeds from sales of this book are going to a wonderful Foundation:

The Pink Ribbon Foundation (Reg. Charity No. 1080839) is a grant making trust with a mission to fund projects and provide financial support to UK charities which relieve the needs of people who are 157 suffering from, or who have been affected by breast cancer or who work to advance the understanding of breast cancer, its early detection and treatment.

The Pink Ribbon Foundation has very little infrastructure, it relies on the hard work given by Trustees, interested parties and its Patrons. This is done in order to maximise the amount, which goes to the charities that benefit from the funds raised.

More information can be found at www.pinkribbonfoundation.org.uk

Find us at **www.Facebook.com/pinkribbonfoundation**

Follow on Twitter @pinkribbonfound

Follow on Instagram @pinkribbonfoundation

Please do follow them as they truly have some great advice and tips to follow.

Printed in Great Britain
by Amazon

17180435R00093